Blue Skies for Lupe

Written & Illustrated by Linda Kurtz Kingsley

Woodbine House   2015

When I was born, I wasn't perfect.
My spine stuck out; my head was too big and
my body too small. Doctors said I'd never walk.

But Mami loved me anyway.

"Lupe," she whispered in my ear,
"Just you wait. You'll do fine."

Mami heard the U.S. doctors were best.

"Maybe they can help Lupe walk," neighbors said.
"Go! What do you have to lose?"

On a night the moon forgot to rise,
we left. Mami carried me
safe in her serape.

We walked for three days and
nights across the Mexican desert.

We crossed into California,
the golden state, into our new life.

Mami got a job.
She followed the crops, picking lettuce,
strawberries, or whatever was ripe.

As she worked, she sang a song
from home—"Cielito Lindo."

It means beautiful little sky,
and the California sky was beautiful:
blue—misted by water pipes for miles and miles.

Blue like the skies in Mexico.

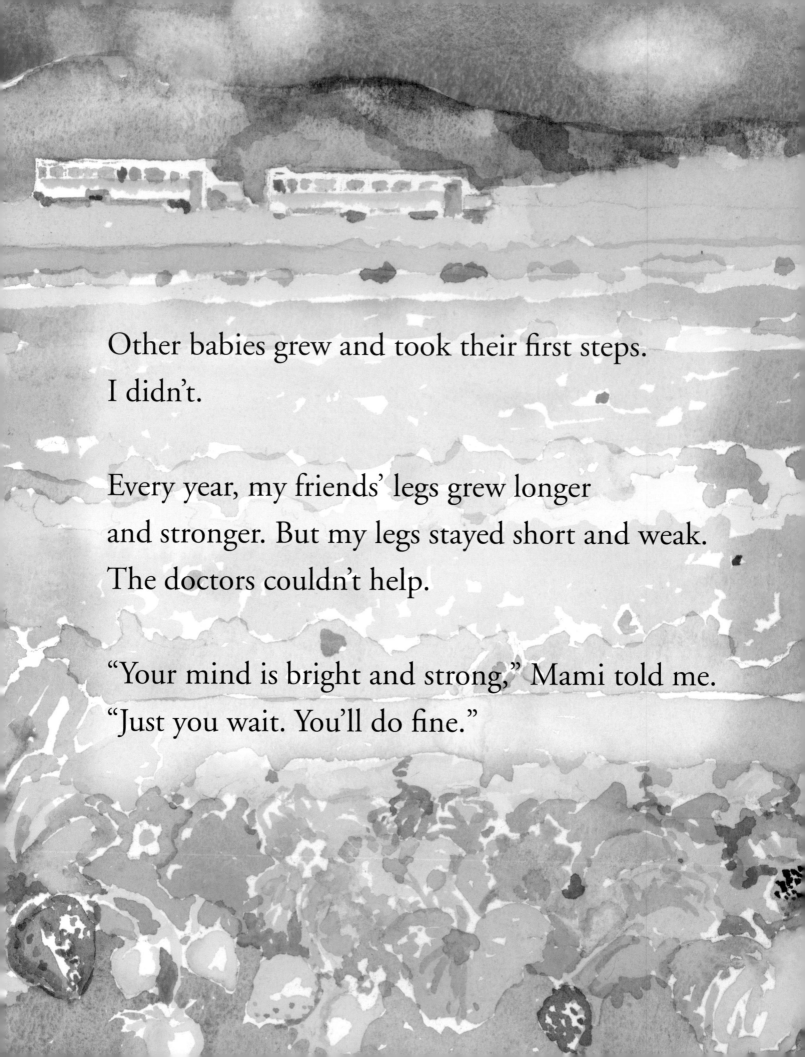

Other babies grew and took their first steps.
I didn't.

Every year, my friends' legs grew longer
and stronger. But my legs stayed short and weak.
The doctors couldn't help.

"Your mind is bright and strong," Mami told me.
"Just you wait. You'll do fine."

When I was six, I started school.
I got my first shiny wheelchair
and an aide named Juanita to
help me.

She pushed my chair.
And she whispered Spanish to
help me understand the English
they spoke in class.

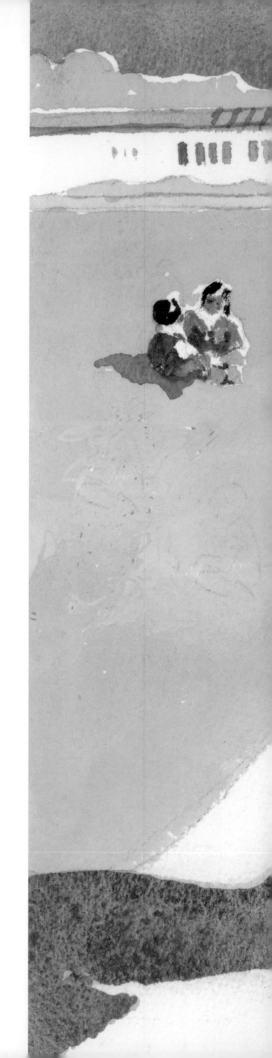

That first day Juanita pushed me
past the gym, where kids were dancing.
We went around the track and
through the crowded classrooms.
How can I do this? I worried.
The kids' curious eyes burned my back.

"You can do almost all the things the other children do," Mami told me that night at dinner.

"You're smarter than you think. You need to do things your way, Lupe. You'll do fine once you learn how. Just you wait."

My classroom was crowded, and I kept bumping into things. One day, my teacher, Mrs. M., was wearing sandals.

"Caramba!" I went over her bare toes with my wheelchair by mistake.

"Ouch!" she yelled.

"Perdón," I said.

"Say sorry," Juanita whispered in my ear. It was on my lips ready to come out, but a giggle came out instead.

Everyone laughed, even Mrs. M. Even me.

On Friday, a special teacher came to help everyone, especially me. She gave me a whiteboard and marker. I couldn't reach the blackboard, but I could do my work on the board and hold it up for Mrs. M. to see.

Next to me, Betty showed me how to do addition. She didn't speak Spanish, but I understood her numbers and her smile. She drew a toe with a big Band Aid on it, and I knew it was Mrs. M.'s. It made me laugh.

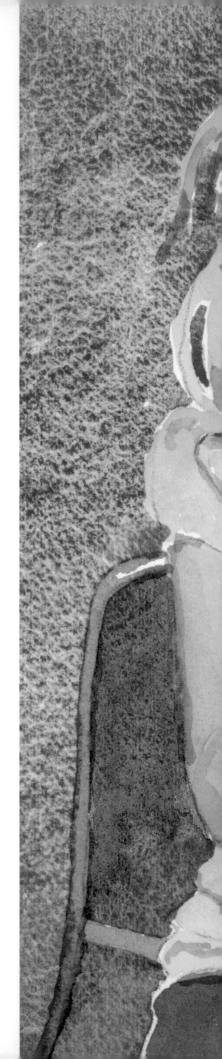

My aide, Juanita, was absent one day,
so I wheeled myself around the
track with the other kids at P.E.

Betty trotted ahead of me yelling,
"Come on! Just do it. You'll be fine."

I kind of understood. I did it all that week.
It made my arms strong and I was fine.

When my teacher saw me joining in,
she got me a mini basket
so I could play basketball
from my chair.

Next I was practicing
hoop shots with the class.

On May fifth,
we had a fiesta for Cinco de Mayo,
a Mexican holiday.

I learned that people in wheelchairs
dance too.

A band played "Cielito Lindo,"
and Mami's proud Spanish voice
rang from the bleachers.

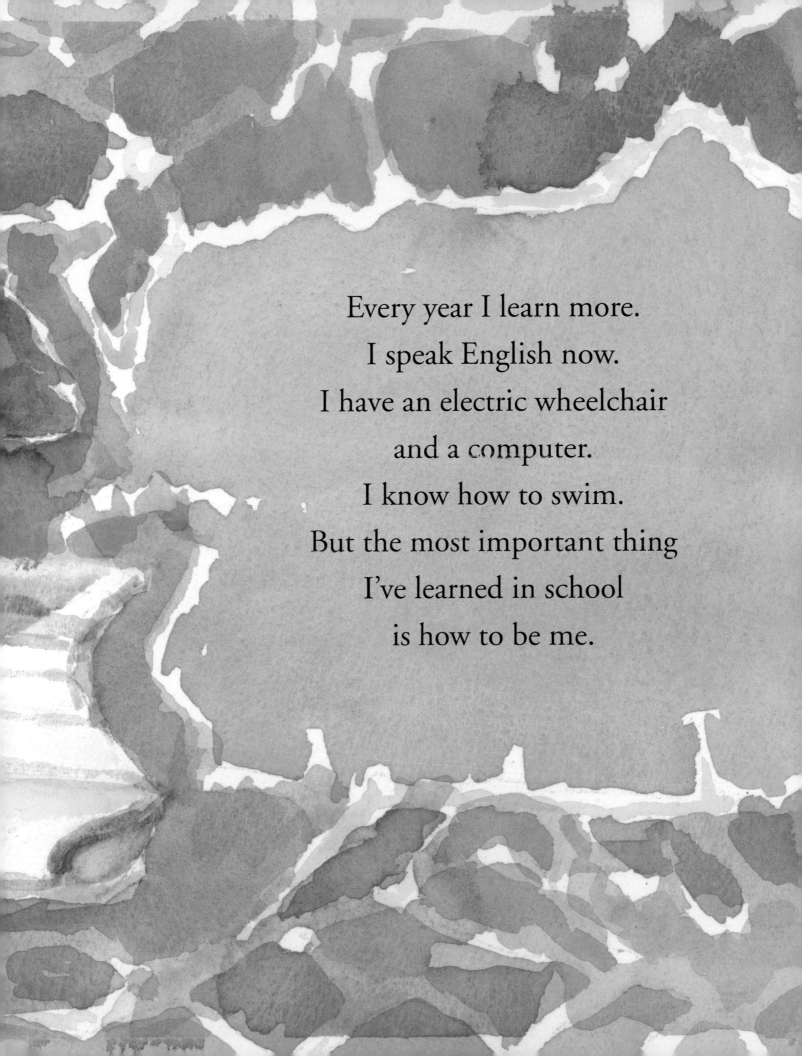

Every year I learn more.
I speak English now.
I have an electric wheelchair
and a computer.
I know how to swim.
But the most important thing
I've learned in school
is how to be me.

I might never walk,
but Mami was right.

I can do almost
anything I want.

And I do fine.

And just like everybody
else, I have dreams.
Beautiful dreams—
Lots and lots of them!

Glossary

SPANISH	ENGLISH
Caramba	Good grief, Darn!
Cielito Lindo	Beautiful little sky
Cinco de Mayo	May fifth
Fiesta	Party
Mami	Mommy
Perdón	Excuse me, Sorry
Serape	Blanket, Shawl

Blue Skies for Lupe is based on a true story. "Lupe" was the first in her family to graduate from high school. Her last year there, she wrote an essay in English class that won her a scholarship to community college. She graduated with a major in computer science. When I interviewed her for this book, she translated for her Spanish-speaking mom, since I don't speak Spanish. Lupe has an electric wheelchair with all the bells and whistles. She plans some day to drive a hand-controlled van. She has a boyfriend and a job. Nothing seems to hold her back.